U.S. Marine Corps Combat Jets

Martha E.H. Rustad
AR B.L.: 3.2
Points: 0.5   MG

MILITARY VEHICLES

★ ★ ★ ★ ★ ★ ★ ★ ★ ★ ★ ★ ★ ★ ★ ★ ★ ★

U.S. MARINE CORPS COMBAT JETS

by Martha E. H. Rustad

★ ★ ★ ★ ★ ★ ★ ★ ★ ★ ★ ★ ★ ★ ★ ★ ★

Reading Consultant:
Barbara J. Fox
Reading Specialist
North Carolina State University

★

Capstone

Mankato, Minnesota

Blazers is published by Capstone Press,
151 Good Counsel Drive, P.O. Box 669, Mankato, Minnesota 56002.
www.capstonepress.com

Library of Congress Cataloging-in-Publication Data
Rustad, Martha E. H. (Martha Elizabeth Hillman), 1975–
    U.S. Marine Corps combat jets / by Martha E. H. Rustad.
    p. cm.—(Blazers. Military vehicles)
    Summary: "Describes U.S. Marine Corps combat jets, including their
design, weapons, equipment, and uses"—Provided by publisher.
    Includes bibliographical references and index.
    ISBN-13: 978-0-7368-6457-2 (hardcover)
    ISBN-10: 0-7368-6457-1 (hardcover)
    1. Harrier (Jet fighter plane)—Juvenile literature. 2. Hornet (Jet fighter
plane)—Juvenile literature. 3. United States. Marine Corps—Aviation—Juvenile
literature. I. Title. II. Series.
UG1242.F5R87 2007
623.74'63—dc22   2006005047

Editorial Credits
Jennifer Besel, editor; Thomas Emery, set designer; Ted Williams, book designer;
    Jo Miller, photo researcher/photo editor

Photo Credits
2004 George Hall/Check Six, 22–23
2005 Keith Chapman/Check Six, 28–29
Corbis/Aero Graphics, Inc., 16–17, 21
Photo by Ted Carlson/Fotodynamics, cover, 4–5, 6–7 (both), 10–11, 14–15,
    18–19, 20, 24–25, 26–27
U.S. Navy Photo/PH1 Jimmy D. Lee, 8–9; PH3 Rodney Jones, 13; PHAA
    Gary L. Johnson III, 12

**Capstone Press thanks Raymond L. Puffer, PhD, Historian, Edwards Air
Force Base, for his assistance in preparing this book.**

1 2 3 4 5 6 11 10 09 08 07 06

TABLE OF CONTENTS

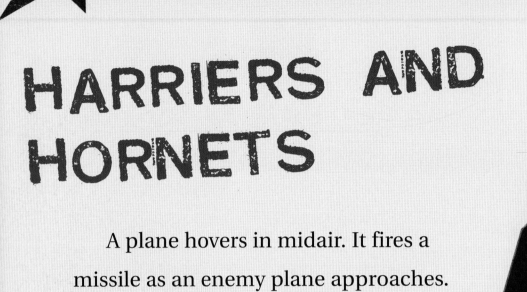

HARRIERS AND HORNETS

A plane hovers in midair. It fires a missile as an enemy plane approaches. Then it speeds off. This unusual flying machine is a Harrier combat jet.

AV-8B HARRIER

F/A-18 HORNET

6

★ ★ ★ ★ ★

U.S. Marine Corps pilots fly the AV-8B Harrier on combat missions. Marine pilots also fly the F/A-18 Hornet. Both planes help Marines who are fighting on the ground.

BLAZER FACT

Both the Harrier and the Hornet can be refueled in the air.

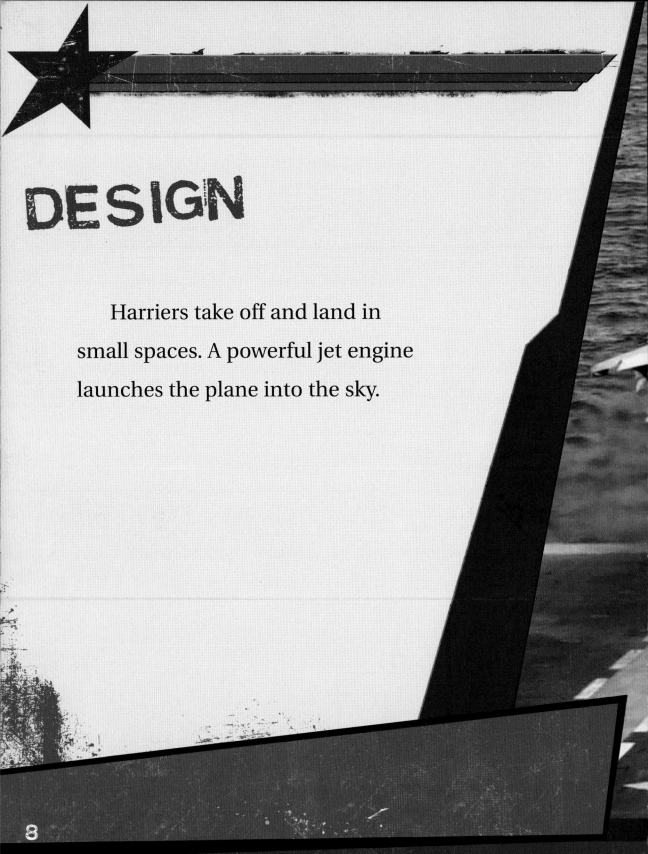

DESIGN

Harriers take off and land in
small spaces. A powerful jet engine
launches the plane into the sky.

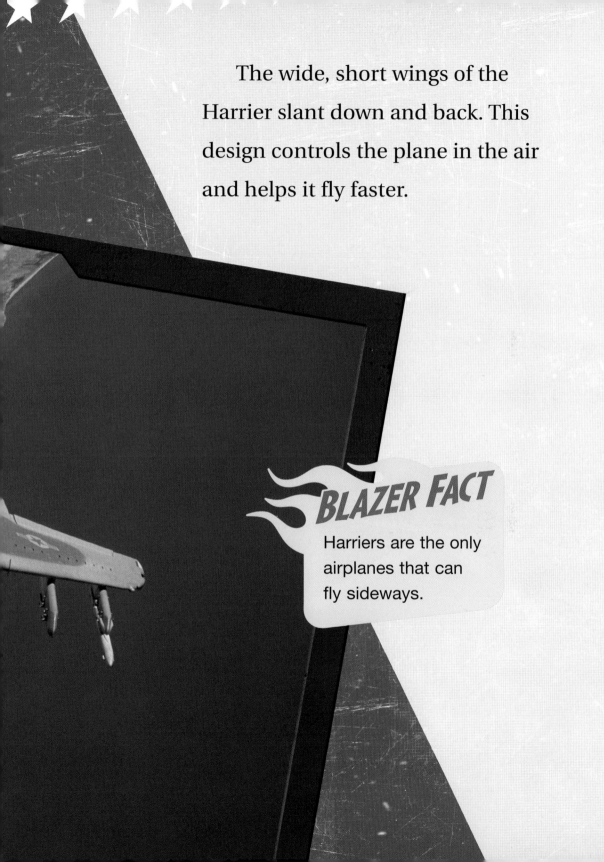

The wide, short wings of the
Harrier slant down and back. This
design controls the plane in the air
and helps it fly faster.

BLAZER FACT

Harriers are the only
airplanes that can
fly sideways.

Most planes need a long runway to
land. But Harriers land vertically, just
like helicopters do.

Two powerful engines push Hornets through the air. Long, thin wings lift the plane during takeoffs.

BLAZER FACT

Hornets fly as fast as 1,290 miles (2,075 kilometers) per hour.

WEAPONS AND EQUIPMENT

Harriers can attack enemy targets on the ground or in the air. They use missiles, machine guns, and bombs.

FUEL DROP TANK

GUIDED BOMB

AIM-9 MISSILES

Hornets carry extra fuel, missiles, and bombs under their wings. Hornets also fire machine guns at air and ground targets.

BLAZER FACT

Hornets have been flown on missions since 1986.

RADAR SCREEN

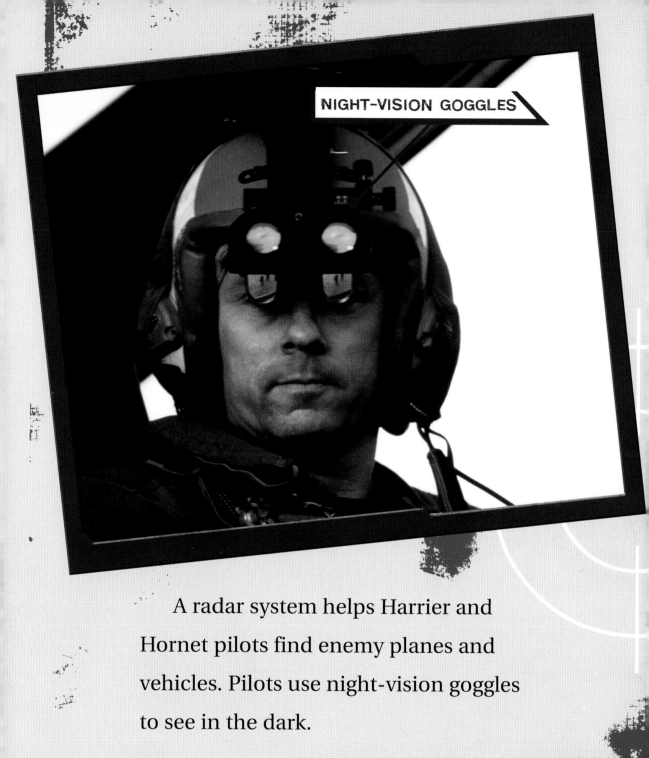

A radar system helps Harrier and
Hornet pilots find enemy planes and
vehicles. Pilots use night-vision goggles
to see in the dark.

AV-8B HARRIER

MISSILE

AIR INLET

COCKPIT

NOSE

TAIL

WING

BOMBS

THE CREW AND ITS MISSIONS

Harrier and Hornet pilots are highly trained. They must be able to fly the planes at very high speeds. They also have to know how to fire weapons at enemy targets.

Marines are the first soldiers to arrive at battles. Harriers and Hornets help Marines carry out missions that keep the United States safe.

SOARING HORNETS!

GLOSSARY

combat (KOM-bat)—fighting between people or armies

goggles (GOG-uhlz)—special glasses that fit tightly around the eyes

hover (HUHV-ur)—to stay in one place in the air

launch (LAWNCH)—to send into action

missile (MISS-uhl)—an explosive weapon that can travel long distances

mission (MISH-uhn)—a military task

radar (RAY-dar)—equipment that uses radio waves to find and guide objects

target (TAR-git)—something that is aimed at or shot at

vertical (VUR-tuh-kuhl)—straight up and down

READ MORE

Doeden, Matt. *The U.S. Marine Corps.* The U.S. Armed Forces. Mankato, Minn.: Capstone Press, 2005.

Lurch, Bruno. *United States Marine Corps.* United States Armed Forces. Chicago: Heinemann, 2004.

INTERNET SITES

FactHound offers a safe, fun way to find Internet sites related to this book. All of the sites on FactHound have been researched by our staff.

Here's how:
1. Visit *www.facthound.com*
2. Choose your grade level.
3. Type in this book ID **0736864571** for age-appropriate sites. You may also browse subjects by clicking on letters, or by clicking on pictures and words.
4. Click on the **Fetch It** button.

FactHound will fetch the best sites for you!

INDEX